# A Taste of Virginia

## Through the Garden Gate

Published by The James River Garden Club

Richmond, Virginia
Organized March 1915
Member, Garden Club of Virginia
Member, The Garden Club of America

Edited by Carroll Wommack Andrews and Clare Osdene Schapiro
Designed by Lauren Murphy Carter

Committee:
Margaret Valentine Brown, Catherine Bradford Bugg, Carrie Baker Dorsey, Carter Hancock Johnston, Lisa Platt Kunz, Gaylen Alders Reynolds, Anne Blackwell Thompson, Laura Provosty Whisnand

Additional copies may be ordered at JamesRiverGardenClub.com

# Dedication

The founders of *A Taste of Virginia*, Legendary chocolate cake at Agecroft Hall & Gardens

This book is dedicated to the innovative, intrepid and indefatigable members of The James River Garden Club who originated this project, and to those who have sustained it through five printings in 38 years. Their efforts in the creation and support of *A Taste of Virginia* have changed the face of the landscape of Virginia forever. They are our mentors, inspiration and beloved friends—and we are forever in their debt.

# Acknowledgements

We thank the individuals and associations for their permission for photographs in this book, the cooks who shared their talents and treasures, and the photography of Madison Waitman. We are grateful for the use of images by Blackwell Botanicals, by James Madison's Montpelier, from *Historic Gardens of Virginia, 1923*, by The James River Garden Club, and, for the map of restored gardens from the Garden Club of Virginia.

# Published by The James River Garden Club

Now in its second century, The James River Garden Club remains committed to its founding mission: to promote interest in gardening, to protect the environment through education and the practice of conservation, and to encourage restoration and civic planting. Proceeds from the sale of this book support these ongoing projects.

# Introduction

E humbly present a new edition of our 1980 cookbook, *A Taste of Virginia*. Gardens, food and history are inextricably tied and provide an invaluable glimpse into our commonwealth. From the most ornate formal garden, to the kitchen gardens of presidents, to the most humble backyard vegetable patch, gardening affords an opportunity to reconnect with the land, but even more, with our essential selves. We think that just as the best tomatoes come straight from the gardens of Virginia, so do the best recipes. It is in this spirit that we return with some tried and true classic recipes, and some new twists on old favorites that build on the pragmatic reality of 21st-century life.

From what is widely viewed as the first American cookbook, *The Virginia Housewife*, by Mrs. Mary Randolph, in 1824, to Edna Lewis' iconic, *The Taste of Country Cooking*, published in 1976, the legacy of Virginia home cooking is the beauty of tradition, and a devotion to authenticity and sustainability.

Our vernacular cooking is an enchanting amalgam of many elements: the native foods that grew here and those brought here by enterprising horticulturalists, such as our first presidents; the ingenuity and talents of enslaved people who led the way in creating our culinary traditions; and, the prodigious bounty of our woods, fields, mountains, rivers, and the Chesapeake Bay.

Now, as then, our cooking is rooted in the seasons. We know that local ingredients harvested at their peak require minimal intervention in the kitchen to render them irresistible. The first shad roe in the spring, the taste of a tomato still warm from the backyard, and the aroma of oysters roasting in the chill autumn air are part of the precious rhythm of Virginia life.

We know that growing your own food brings beauty and meaning to daily life, and we know the value of honoring diversity—in culture and in the garden. Above all, we know that nothing is more emblematic of a taste of Virginia than slowing down, cooking real food in season and sharing the love and ritual of dining together.

While merely a "taste" of some of the culinary delights found in this very special corner of the world, our hope is that *A Taste of Virginia: Through the Garden Gate* will intrigue and delight you, and whet your appetite for gardening and cooking, but more importantly, for exploring all that the commonwealth has to offer.

With this in mind, we warmly welcome you to join us, "through the garden gate".

# Table of Contents

Blackwell Botanicals

Blackwell Botanicals

## Fall

Surry country ham and cheese puffs   28

Molly's Brunswick stew   28

Royal Pippin shrub   28

Tidewater pickled oysters   29

Topping oyster dressing   30

Pear chopped salad   31

Molly's popovers   31

Dove or quail   31

Pork with apple cider sauce   32

Barbour-q sauce   32

Brussels sprouts with chestnuts   32

Bourbon sweet potato pudding   33

Legendary chocolate cake   34

Blue Ridge apple cake   35

Ginger pear crumble   35

Blackwell Botanicals

## Winter

Crab Mornay   38

Cocktail cheese wafers   38

Westmoreland Club eggnog   38

Urbanna oyster stew   39

Stuffed Winter squash   40

Eastern Shore sweet potato biscuits   40

Venison chili   41

Beaten or thin biscuits   41

Hash   41

Pound cake   42

Peppermint ice cream   42

    with dark chocolate sauce

Eggnog bread pudding with hard sauce   43

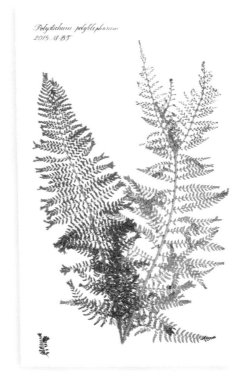

Blackwell Botanicals

pring

Opposite Page: Colonial Williamsburg

# Pickled shrimp  Makes 6 servings

*This old-fashioned favorite is, perhaps, the perfect last-minute hors d'oeuvre.*

¼ cup extra virgin olive oil

⅓ cup fresh lemon juice

⅓ cup white wine vinegar

1 T whole mustard seeds

1 tsp celery seed

1 bulb fennel, cored and sliced thinly

½ medium white onion, sliced thinly

¼ cup capers

¼ cup flat leaf parsley, chopped

salt and pepper to taste

1 ½ pound fresh wild shrimp; shelled, cleaned, cooked, and chilled

6 whole bay leaves

1 lemon, sliced thinly

Toothpicks or cocktail forks for serving

In a large bowl combine all ingredients except shrimp, bay leaves and lemon slices. Stir well. Add shrimp, bay leaves, and lemon slices and toss gently. Refrigerate for a minimum of one hour.

### THREE WAYS TO COOK SHAD ROE

Serve with bacon and lemon wedges, boiled new potatoes with chopped parsley or chives, and asparagus Hollandaise.

I. Fry in bacon grease in iron skillet. Turn once. Beware spattering (20-30 minutes).

II. Put roe in iron skillet, cover with bacon strips. Put in cold oven. Turn oven to 375°, bake until firm and brown but not dry (30-60 minutes, depending on size). This is the easiest method.

III. Wrap roe in waxed paper, fry in bacon grease on top of stove over medium heat. For some reason the paper doesn't burn.

Recipe from the original *A Taste of Virginia*

# Irvington smash  Makes 4 servings

*There's nothing like strawberries at their peak. A rocking chair at the river is the perfect spot to celebrate the arrival of spring. Be sure to plant mint in a pot so it doesn't overtake your garden.*

2 cups fresh strawberries, hulled and sliced

4 T fresh lemon juice

3 T honey syrup

10 leaves fresh mint

1 cup Cirrus Vodka

2 cups soda

Additional mint for garnish

In a pitcher, muddle strawberries, lemon juice, honey syrup and mint. Add the vodka and soda and stir well. Pour into tall, ice-filled glasses and garnish with mint.

Honey Syrup:

Heat equal parts honey and water until honey is dissolved.

Tuckahoe Plantation

# Rockfish with garden sauce  Makes 4 - 6 servings

*A new look at recipes from our 1980 original. The versatile garden sauce is a perfect accompaniment for any cold meat, fish, crudité, or salad.*

## Garden sauce

Zest of 1 lemon

1 T lemon juice, or more for thinner sauce

1 cup Duke's Mayonnaise

½ cup sour cream

½ cup plain Greek yogurt

fresh herbs: 2 T each of tarragon, chives, dill and flat leaf parsley. Chop coarsely.

Salt and pepper to taste

Put lemon juice, zest, mayonnaise, sour cream, yogurt, and fresh herbs in blender. Pulse until well blended. Add salt and pepper. Cover and chill for 30 minutes to allow flavors to meld.

2 pounds rockfish fillets

Extra virgin olive oil

Salt and pepper

1 lemon cut into thin slices

Sprigs of tarragon, dill and flat leaf parsley

2 T dry white wine, divided into individual pouches

Parchment paper

## Rockfish

Preheat oven to 400 degrees. Place each fillet in the middle of a piece of parchment paper twice its size on a baking sheet. Brush fillets with olive oil. Add salt and pepper. Place lemon slices and herbs on fillets. Bring sides of parchment together to create a pouch around fillet. Seal pouches by rolling and crimping edges of parchment except for last two inches. Add a little wine to each pouch. Finish sealing parchment. (Use moistened fingers to seal parchment.) Bake 10 minutes per inch of thickness of the fillets. Remove fillets from parchment pouches and serve with garden sauce.

# Molly's Sally Lunn bread  Makes 6 - 8 servings

*A true Virginia treasure from one of our garden club treasures. In the good old days, Sally Lunn was made by hand and included instructions to "beat vigorously with a wooden spoon." We make ours in a stand mixer with the dough-hook attachment. And it works perfectly.*

⅓ cup warm water (between 105-110 degrees)

2 ¼ ounce packages of active dry yeast

1 tsp sugar, and ⅓ cup of sugar, divided

⅔ cup milk, scalded and cooled to lukewarm

½ cup butter and 2 T, divided, softened to room temperature

4 eggs at room temperature

1 tsp salt

4 cups all-purpose flour

Butter for serving

Place ⅓ cup of warm water in a large Pyrex measuring cup. Add the yeast and 1 teaspoon of sugar and stir lightly to mix. Let stand for 5 minutes to proof. Add milk, mix and set aside.

In a stand mixer, cream ½ cup butter until light, and add remaining ⅓ cup of sugar mixing until fluffy. Add eggs, one at a time, beating well after each addition. Mix in salt. Add the flour, 1 cup at a time, alternating with ⅓ of the yeast mixture, beginning and ending with flour. Beat vigorously until smooth and elastic. Place in a well-buttered bowl, cover with a cloth, and let rise in a warm, draft-free place until doubled in bulk, about 1 - 2 hours.

Punch dough down and transfer to a buttered and floured 3-quart crown bundt pan or tube pan. Smear remaining softened butter on top of dough, if using a tube pan. Cover and let rise in a warm place for 30 - 45 minutes until doubled in bulk.

Preheat oven to 350 degrees. When dough has risen, bake about 30 minutes until well browned, and bread is hollow sounding when tapped. Unmold and serve hot with lots of butter.

Colonial Williamsburg

Annie duPont Formal Garden at James Madison's Montpelier, by Kendall Madigan

### VIRGINIA HAM

Find a pot big enough to hold a 3-5 year old ham weighing 12-18 lbs. Scrub ham with stiff brush under running water. Cover with cold water and soak overnight. (A younger ham may not need soaking.) Put ham in boiler, cover with cold water, bring to simmer. Simmer until end bone is loose—5 hours to all day, depending on size and age of ham. Take off heat and leave in cooking water until cool. Remove ham to board or platter, peel off skin (messy job), leave layer of fat. Score fat in diamond pattern. Cover top thickly with mixture of fine breadcrumbs and brown sugar. Pat smooth all over ham. Stick clove in each diamond. Bake at 350° until brown. Watch carefully—sugar burns easily. Store in cool place, covered with plastic.

Recipe from the original A *Taste of Virginia*

# Chutney chicken salad Makes 4 servings

*While not Mrs. Mary Randolph's original recipe, we serve this with Richmond Rice Salad for easy and delicious spring luncheons.*

¾ cup Duke's Mayonnaise

½ cup Virginia Chutney Co. Sweet Peach chutney

4 tsp curry powder

4 cups cooked chicken, shredded

Salt and pepper to taste

½ cup chopped green onion

½ cup chopped Virginia peanuts

In large bowl combine all ingredients, chill and serve.

Tuckahoe Plantation

# Tuckahoe rack of lamb  Makes 4-6 servings

*Perfect for Easter, or any spring feast.*

2 racks of lamb

6 T olive oil, divided

Salt and pepper

1 cup fresh parsley leaves, chopped finely

½ cup fresh mint leaves, chopped finely

1 ½ T fresh rosemary, minced

4 cloves garlic, minced

Freshly grated zest of 1 lemon

1 - 1 ½ cup freshly made bread crumbs

3 T Dijon mustard

Mint sauce or mint jelly for serving

Preheat oven to 450 degrees. Place lamb fat side up in a roasting pan. Rub half the olive oil on top and sprinkle with salt and pepper. Roast for 10 minutes and remove from oven. In a medium bowl, mix herbs, garlic and zest, salt and pepper to taste. Add remaining olive oil and the bread crumbs and mix well. Thickly brush the mustard over the top of the meat. Place the bread-crumb mixture on top and using the back of a fork, press down to compress it.

Return lamb immediately to the oven and roast for an additional 15 minutes or until a meat thermometer inserted into the thickest part of the meat is 125 degrees for rare or 135 degrees for medium rare.

Remove and tent the lamb with foil to rest for 15 minutes before cutting into chops and serving.

# Wild mushroom and asparagus tart   Makes 6 servings

*Easy and elegant.*

I Never-Fail Pie Crust, blind baked in a 10-inch tart pan (below)

1 T unsalted butter

2 shallots, peeled and thinly sliced

½ pound wild mushrooms, coarsely chopped

1 bunch asparagus, tough ends removed, chopped diagonally into 1-inch pieces, about 2 cups

Salt and pepper to taste

3 eggs

1 cup cream or half-and-half

1 tsp Dijon mustard

½ pound Gruyere cheese, grated and divided

Blind bake the crust in a 10-inch tart pan, see below.

Preheat oven to 350 degrees. Melt butter in a large skillet over medium heat. Add shallots and cook, stirring for 2 minutes until translucent. Add mushrooms and cook stirring for about 8 minutes until mushrooms have given up their moisture. Add asparagus, salt and pepper, and cook for 2 minutes, stirring. Asparagus will be bright green. Remove from heat.

In a medium bowl, combine eggs, cream, and mustard. Whisk well.

Put half the cheese on the crust followed by the vegetable mixture. Pour in egg mixture. Top with remaining cheese. Bake about 30 minutes or until almost set. Allow to cool for 15 minutes. Remove from tart pan and serve.


# Never-fail pie crust   Makes 3 - 4 large pie crusts

*A dream come true—and so easy! It comes together in about five minutes and freezes beautifully. We usually make four at a time.*

4 cups all-purpose flour

2 tsp salt

1 ¾ cups unsalted butter, non-hydrogenated vegetable shortening or Crisco, chilled

½ cup cold water

1 T apple cider vinegar

1 egg

In a large bowl combine flour and salt. Cut butter into flour mixture until crumbly.
In a separate bowl, mix water, vinegar and egg. Add to the flour mixture and mix well.

Separate into 3 - 4 balls. If using immediately, refrigerate for at least an hour before rolling. If saving for later, form into disks, wrap separately in plastic wrap, and place in a freezer bag and freeze. Allow to thaw in the refrigerator for 3 hours before using.

To blind bake: Preheat the oven to 350. Roll out pastry and place in desired pan. Place a layer of aluminum foil on the top and weight it with either pastry weights or dried beans. Bake for 10 minutes. Remove the weights and foil and bake for 10 minutes more until the crust is lightly browned. Remove and cool on a rack for about 20 minutes before the final baking.

# Richmond rice salad   Makes 4 servings

*A splendid side dish to accompany most anything.*

2 cups cooked, cooled long-grain rice

¾ cup shredded carrots, preferably a mix of colors

¼ cup May peas, blanched or lightly cooked frozen peas

¼ cup sliced scallions

1 red bell pepper, diced

¼ cup flat leaf parsley, chopped

vinaigrette

¼ cup Virginia peanuts, lightly toasted and chopped

### Lemon dill vinaigrette

1 tsp Dijon mustard

2 T fresh lemon juice

½ cup extra virgin olive oil

1 T chopped fresh dill

Salt and pepper

Combine rice, carrots, peas, scallions, red pepper, and parsley. Mix to combine. To make vinaigrette spoon mustard in shallow bowl, whisk in lemon juice and while continuing to whisk slowly stream in olive oil. Add dill, salt and pepper. Add vinaigrette to salad. Toss, cover and refrigerate for at least an hour to allow flavors to meld. Fold in peanuts.

# Cheese grits soufflé, night and day   Makes 6 servings

*Dressed up with snipped fresh chives and a local cheese, these grits are an elegant accompaniment to beef tenderloin. Or, use a sharp cheddar with bits of smoky sausage for your favorite overnight guests after you've danced the night away. Byrd Mill has been milling Virginia grains since 1740.*

4 eggs, plus 2 egg whites

1 quart milk

1 tsp salt

4 T unsalted butter, divided

1 cup Byrd Mill Old-Tyme White or other grits, not instant

½ tsp ground white pepper

3 cups shredded cheese

Salt and pepper

In a small bowl, beat eggs and egg whites until well combined. Set aside.

In a saucepan, bring milk to a heavy simmer. Do not boil. Add salt and 1 tablespoon butter. Gradually whisk in grits. Reduce heat to medium low and continue to cook, stirring occasionally, for 25 minutes. Remove from heat. Add remaining butter, white pepper and cheese and stir to combine. Mix in eggs well.

Preheat oven to 350 degrees.

Pour into deep, buttered baking or soufflé dish. Bake for about 50 minutes or until golden and just set.

Lewis Ginter Botanical Garden

# Garden Week strawberry shortcake Makes 6 servings

*A true Virginia classic made for today's table. The mascarpone cheese adds delightful depth to the whipped cream and allows it to be made hours, or even days, in advance.*

## Mascarpone cream

¾ cup whipping cream

1 8-ounce container of mascarpone cheese

2 T sugar

2 tsp vanilla

Whip cream and mascarpone together with an electric mixer. Add sugar and vanilla and continue beating just until soft peaks form. Cover and refrigerate for up to 3 days.

## Strawberry shortcake

4 cups fresh strawberries, rinsed, hulled and sliced in half and sugared to taste

2 cups all-purpose flour

3 T sugar

1 T baking powder

¼ tsp salt

½ cup cold unsalted butter

1 large egg, beaten

⅔ cup half-and-half

Mint for garnish

Prepare strawberries and refrigerate for at least two hours.

Preheat oven to 450 degrees. In a large mixing bowl, combine the flour, sugar, baking powder, and salt. Mix well. Add the butter, cutting it into the mixture until crumbly. In a small bowl, whisk the egg and half-and-half together. Add to the flour mixture and stir just until a dough forms. Turn the dough onto a floured surface and knead briefly. Pat the dough to about 3/4-inch thick, then, with a floured 3-inch biscuit cutter, cut out 6 biscuits. Place them on an ungreased baking sheet and bake on the upper rack of the oven until slightly brown on top, about 10 minutes.

Split the biscuits in half and spoon the berries and then the mascarpone cream onto the bottoms of the biscuits. Place the tops back on, and serve while still warm. Garnish with fresh mint.

 ummer

Opposite Page: Monticello, Top: Falls of the James River, Bottom Left: The University of Virginia

# Falls-of-the-James fizz

Makes 8 servings

*Richmond boasts the best urban white water in the country. Make this refreshing limeade cocktail after a day on the river.*

½ to 1 cup honey syrup to taste

Zest of 2 limes

1 cup fresh lime juice

1 ½ cups Commonwealth Gin

6 cups soda water

Combine all ingredients in a large pitcher. Stir well and pour into tall ice-filled glasses. Garnish with a slice of lime.

Honey syrup

Heat equal parts honey and water until honey is dissolved.

The Low Line, Richmond

# Fig and blue cheese crostada  Makes 6 - 8 servings

*This easy, rustic tart is a great way to enjoy figs as they ripen in late summer.*

2 T unsalted butter

2 T extra virgin olive oil

2 large sweet onions, thinly sliced

1 T fresh thyme leaves, minced

1 large Never-Fail Pie Crust, (page 13) rolled to an ⅛-inch thick rectangle

1 T balsamic vinegar

6 ounces mild blue cheese, crumbled

12 ripe, fresh figs, quartered and stems removed

3 T pine nuts

Preheat oven to 350 degrees. Heat butter and olive oil in a large skillet over medium-low heat. Add onion and thyme. Stir occasionally until deeply browned, about 30 minutes. In the meantime, place the pastry on parchment paper on a rimmed sheet pan. Push the edges up to create a ½ inch rim. Bake pastry for 20 minutes. Remove the onions from the heat. Stir in balsamic, scraping up any brown bits. Spoon onions into cooled pastry, followed by the cheese. Place figs on top with stem ends up. Sprinkle on pine nuts. Put back in the oven for about 5 minutes so that cheese melts a bit. Slice and serve immediately.

The Market at Grelen

## Gazpacho  Makes 12 servings

*A recipe for "Gaspacho" first appeared in Mary Randolph's 1824 cookbook, The Virginia House-wife, the first American cookbook. Our flexible version can be adjusted to include any vegetables or herbs in your garden.*

64 ounces low-sodium tomato juice

1 cup tarragon vinegar

2 T Worcestershire sauce

2 cups sweet onions, finely chopped

1 cucumber, seeded and coarsely chopped

2 cups coarsely chopped celery

1 large yellow pepper, seeded and coarsely chopped

1 ½ cups corn kernels, fresh or frozen, cooked and drained

4 cloves of garlic, peeled and minced

4 large ripe, fresh, heirloom tomatoes, peeled and coarsely chopped

4 T chopped fresh chives

3 T chopped fresh flat leaf parsley

Salt and pepper to taste

Combine all ingredients. Mix well and chill for at least 4 hours and serve.

## CRAB CAKES

2 cups fresh crabmeat
1 egg, beaten lightly
1 small onion, minced

2 tablespoons mayonnaise
breadcrumbs from 1 hard roll
salt, pepper, pinch Old Bay or mace

Mix all ingredients gently, shape into patties, fry in butter or margarine. Makes 6 or 8 crab cakes, depending on size.

Recipe from the original A *Taste of Virginia*

# Chesapeake Bay crab soufflé  Makes 2 - 4 servings

¾ cup of finely grated Asiago cheese, divided

3 T minced shallots

3 T butter

3 T flour

1 cup milk

Salt and pepper

½ cup grated Gruyere cheese

3 egg yolks

¾ cup fresh lump crab meat

6 egg whites

Pinch of cream of tartar

⅛ tsp of salt

Preheat oven to 400 degrees. Butter a 6-cup soufflé dish and dust with ¼ cup Asiago cheese. Reserve remaining cheese. Cook shallots in butter on medium low for several minutes. Stir in flour, and cook for 2 minutes. Gradually blend in milk, salt and pepper. Cook, stirring until thick and smooth. Add Gruyere, stir and remove from heat and cool slightly. Beat in egg yolks one at a time. Fold in crab meat. Cool.

In a bowl, beat egg whites until frothy. Add cream of tartar and salt. Beat until stiff peaks form. Gently fold into soufflé base. Pour the mixture into the prepared dish and sprinkle with remaining grated Asiago cheese. Place on rack in lower third of oven. Immediately lower the oven to 375 degrees and cook for approximately 25-30 minutes.

# Piney River cornbread  Makes 6-8 servings

*Woodson's Mill began milling cornmeal in Virginia in 1794. Traditionally, cornbread in Virginia is made without sugar and corn kernels. We'll let you decide.*

4 T unsalted butter

1 ½ cups coarse cornmeal

3 T sugar or maple syrup (optional)

¾ tsp baking soda

1 tsp salt

2 eggs

1½ cup buttermilk

1 ½ cups fresh corn kernels (optional)

Butter and AR's Hot Southern Honey for serving

Preheat the oven to 425 degrees. Add butter to a 10-inch cast iron skillet and put in oven until butter is lightly browned. Swirl butter to coat pan and set aside. Combine dry ingredients and wet ingredients in separate bowls. Pour wet ingredients into dry and combine gently. Pour butter into batter and stir. Fold in corn. Pour into skillet and bake for 20 minutes. Slather with butter and AR's Hot Southern Honey.

Dockside at Topping

# Tomato aspic with basil mayonnaise  Makes 8 servings

*Delicious accompanied with chilled crab or shrimp, sliced or deviled egg, and sliced avocado.*

Canola oil for preparing mold or dish

1 T (2 envelopes) unflavored gelatin

4 cups fresh or canned unsalted tomato juice, divided

1 T sugar

2 T freshly squeezed lemon juice

1 tsp onion juice (obtained from grating onion)

Sea salt and freshly ground pepper to taste

Basil sprig for garnish

Lightly oil a 4-cup, non-reactive mold or loaf pan. In a small bowl, soften the gelatin in ½ cup of the tomato juice. In a medium saucepan, heat remaining tomato juice until it begins to simmer. Remove from heat. Whisk in gelatin mixture and sugar. Once dissolved, add remaining ingredients and stir. Pour into mold and chill at least 12 hours. Unmold, slice and serve with basil mayonnaise and garnish with a basil sprig.

## Basil mayonnaise  Makes 1 ½ cups

*Serve with aspic, on sliced tomatoes, or as a sandwich spread.*

2 T olive oil

1 cup Duke's Mayonnaise

Zest of 1 lemon

1 tsp lemon juice

1 cup fresh basil leaves, tightly packed

Combine all ingredients except basil in a food processor or blender. Mix well, then add basil and puree until smooth and bright green. Chill for several hours before serving.

# Hanover tomato thyme jam
Makes about 1 pint

*When it's tomato time, it's time for spicy tomato jam—good on everything from sandwiches and burgers to ham biscuits.*

2 pounds ripe fresh tomatoes, cored and coarsely chopped

½ cup sugar

Grated zest and juice of 2 limes

½ tsp ground cinnamon

½ tsp ground cloves

½ tsp ground cumin

1 tsp salt and freshly ground pepper

Leaves from 5 stems of fresh thyme, or to taste

Combine tomatoes, sugar, lime zest and juice, cinnamon, cloves, cumin, salt and pepper in a heavy saucepan. Bring to a boil over medium heat while stirring. Reduce heat and simmer uncovered, stirring occasionally, until it has the consistency of thick jam, about an hour. Remove from heat, cool, add thyme and refrigerate until ready to serve.

# Summer squash
Makes 6 servings

*While cymlings, or pattypan squash, were Thomas Jefferson's favorite, this recipe makes use of the crookneck squash: more common today. A quick, easy and delicious paean to summer.*

3 T unsalted butter or bacon fat

1 large sweet onion, halved and sliced thinly

1 red bell pepper, cut into ½-inch dice

1 ½ pounds yellow summer squash, cut into ½-inch rounds

Salt and lots of freshly ground black pepper

2 T fresh chives (optional)

Place butter or bacon fat in a large, heavy skillet over medium heat and allow to melt. Add the onion and red bell pepper and cook, stirring, until the onion is translucent, about 5 - 8 minutes. Add the squash and continue stirring until the squash is translucent, about 10 minutes. Add salt and pepper to taste. Remove from heat, sprinkle with chives and serve.

# Piedmont corn pudding
Makes 4-6 servings

*The perfect dish when corn is at its peak.*

2 eggs

1 cup half-and-half

2 T brown sugar

1 T chopped fresh chives

A pinch of freshly grated nutmeg

Salt and pepper to taste

3 cups corn kernels, from about 10 ears

Preheat oven to 350 degrees. Butter a 4-6 cup shallow baking dish. Beat liquid ingredients until combined. Add sugar, chives, nutmeg, salt and pepper. Stir in corn. Bake until light golden and slightly firm to the touch, about 35-45 minutes.

The Executive Mansion

# Pimento cheese tomato pie  Makes 4-6 servings

*A perennial summer hit. Pimento cheese is traditionally made with half-white, half-yellow cheese. Make it your way.*

## Pimento cheese

1 ½ pounds extra-sharp cheddar cheese, grated

1 4-ounce jar chopped pimentos, drained

¾ cup Duke's Mayonnaise

2 tsp Worcestershire sauce

1 tsp Dijon mustard

Black pepper to taste (optional)

Hot sauce to taste (optional)

Combine all of the ingredients and, using a fork, stir and mash the mixture until it forms a chunky spread. Chill.

## Pie

1 Never-Fail Pie Crust, blind baked, (page 13)

3 large tomatoes, sliced, salted and allowed to dry on paper towels for one hour before assembly

1 large sweet onion, peeled and sliced very thinly into rounds

One-half recipe pimento cheese, as above

Preheat oven to 350 degrees. In the pie crust, layer tomatoes and half the sliced onions then dollops of pimento cheese on top, about a tablespoon at a time. Repeat. Bake for 45 minutes until brown and bubbling. Remove from oven, allow to set for 5 minutes, before serving.

The Blue Ridge Mountains

# Botetourt butterbean salad   Makes 6 servings

*Fresh herbs enliven a salad of our favorite summer legume.*

2 cups freshly shelled butterbeans, cooked and cooled

⅓ cup pickled red onion, chopped (see below)

2 tsp chopped dill

2 tsp chopped flat leaf parsley

1 cup cherry tomatoes, halved

¼ cup minced green onion

Juice of one lemon

2 T extra virgin olive oil

Combine butterbeans, pickled onion, herbs, tomatoes and green onions in a bowl. Toss gently. Add the juice of one lemon and drizzle with olive oil. Salt and pepper to taste.

# Pickled red onions   Makes one pint

*Quick pickles can be made from most any vegetable you find at your farmers market. Try beets, carrots, cucumbers, green beans, okra, or tomatoes. Experiment with different amounts of sugar, spices and herbs. Try additions like cloves, allspice, mustard seed, coriander, caraway, dill seed, garlic, tarragon, or thyme.*

1 cup water

1 cup white wine vinegar

2 T sugar

1 tsp kosher salt

½ tsp peppercorns

1 pound red onions, halved, peeled and sliced thinly

Bring first 5 ingredients to a boil. Reduce heat and let simmer for 5 minutes. Cool slightly. Place vegetables in containers and add liquid to cover. Let stand at room temperature for one hour stirring occasionally, and serve. Cover and refrigerate any leftovers.

# A fool for summer   Makes 6 servings

*A completely easy take on Peach Melba.*

3 cups ripe, local peaches, sliced into bite-sized pieces

1 cup ripe raspberries

4 T sugar

1 ½ cups crumbled Almond Shortbread Bars (page 25)

1 batch Mascarpone Cream, (page 15)

⅓ cup raspberry preserves

In a large bowl combine peaches and raspberries with 4 tablespoons sugar. Allow to macerate, for one hour, stirring occasionally. Fold cookies into mascarpone-cream and barely swirl in preserves. In a large glass bowl or individual glasses, layer cream mixture and fruit. Chill until serving.

# Almond shortbread bars  Makes 16 servings

2 cups all-purpose flour

½ cup sugar

¼ tsp salt

2 sticks unsalted butter, cold and cut into chunks and additional for greasing pan

1 ½ tsp grated lemon zest

½ tsp almond extract

2 T sugar for sprinkling over the top

Preheat the oven to 350 degrees. Press foil or parchment paper across a 9-by-9 inch square baking pan allowing the edges to hang over the sides by an inch all around. Grease the foil with butter. In medium bowl, combine the flour, sugar, salt, butter, lemon zest, and almond extract, and mix until crumbly. Press the dough into the pan. Sprinkle sugar over the top and bake for 25 to 30 minutes until just brown around the edges. Remove from oven and let cool on wire rack for an hour. Remove from pan using the foil handles and cut into 16 bars (or, 8, to make 4 ice cream sandwiches).

# Blackberry-peach buckle  Makes 8 servings
*A charming old-fashioned country dessert.*

## Topping

4 T cold unsalted butter, cut into chunks

½ cup sugar

⅓ cup all-purpose flour

½ tsp ground cinnamon

½ tsp grated nutmeg

¼ cup sliced almonds

## Batter

1 ⅓ cup all-purpose flour

¼ tsp baking powder

½ tsp salt

12 T unsalted butter, softened

¾ cup sugar

1 tsp vanilla extract

½ tsp almond extract

3 large eggs

2 cups blackberries

2 large peaches (about 9 ounces total) peeled, pitted and cut into 1-inch pieces

Vanilla-bean ice cream for serving

First, make topping: With your fingertips, blend all of the ingredients together in a small bowl until large clumps form.  Refrigerate.

Place rack in middle of oven and preheat to 350 degrees.  Butter a 10-by-2-inch round cake pan or a 2-quart baking dish. Stir together flour, baking powder and salt and set aside.

Cream butter and sugar together in a large bowl with an electric mixer. Add vanilla and almond extract, then eggs one at a time, beating well after each one.  Stir in flour mixture until just combined.  Fold in blackberries and peaches. Spread batter in buttered pan and layer topping evenly over it.  Bake until a wooden skewer inserted in the center comes out clean, and the topping is crunchy and brown, about 60 minutes.  Serve warm with ice cream.

all

Opposite Page: Westover Plantation, Top Right: Chickens at Shirley Plantation, Bottom: The James River at Westover Plantation

# Surry country ham and cheese puffs · Makes 16 puffs

*A perfect hot hors d'oeuvre, or accompaniment for salad and soup.*

½ cup milk

1 stick (8 tablespoons) unsalted butter, cut into pieces

½ tsp salt

1 cup all-purpose flour

4 large eggs, at room temperature

1 teaspoon dry mustard powder

Pinch of cayenne pepper (optional)

1 cup freshly grated sharp cheddar or Parmigiano-Reggiano cheese

½ cup Edwards Country Ham, thinly sliced and chopped

Preheat oven to 400 degrees. Combine milk, ½ cup water, butter, and salt in a medium-sized heavy saucepan and bring to a boil over high heat. Reduce to moderate, add the flour all at once and beat the mixture with a wooden spoon until it pulls away from the sides of the pan and forms a ball. Transfer to a bowl. Beat in the eggs one at a time and then stir in the mustard powder, cayenne, cheese, and ham. Put parchment paper on a large baking sheet (or two smaller baking sheets) and drop batter in 16 mounds, about 1 ½ inches in diameter, leaving ½ inch between puffs. Bake in the top third of the oven for 20 minutes or until golden. Serve immediately, or turn oven off and open the door slightly to keep them warm for up to 1 hour.

# Molly's Brunswick stew · Makes 12 servings

*Virginia's very own creation, made easier for today by our beloved Molly.*

2 T vegetable oil

2 large sweet onions, chopped

4 ribs celery, chopped

1 28-ounce can tomatoes

Salt and pepper to taste

2 ½ quarts unsalted chicken stock

1 T Worcestershire sauce

1 tsp smoked paprika

The meat from 1 rotisserie chicken shredded, with skin and bones discarded

½ pound Edwards Country Ham, chopped

3 cups fresh or frozen white corn kernels

3 cups fresh or frozen butterbeans (lima beans)

4 white potatoes, peeled and cut into 1-inch dice

Place the oil in a large stock pot and heat to medium. Add the onions and celery and cook, stirring, until translucent, about 8 minutes. Add the tomatoes, salt and pepper, the stock, Worcestershire and smoked paprika. Simmer for 10 minutes. Add the chicken, ham, corn, butter beans, and potatoes. Stir well and simmer uncovered until potatoes are cooked and stew is very thick, 40 minutes or longer.

# Royal Pippin shrub · Makes 1 drink

*A drink fit for a queen. Queen Victoria was so taken with Albemarle Pippin apples that she presented the grower with a set of china, still treasured today.*

1 ½ ounces Ironclad Bourbon

Thin slice of pippin or other local apple

4 ounces Albemarle CiderWorks Royal Pippin Apple Cider

1½ ounces Mother Shrub Drinking Vinegar, Ginger

Fill a tall glass with ice. Pour in bourbon, shrub and cider. Stir. Garnish with a thin apple slice.

Pumpkins at Shirley Plantation

# Tidewater pickled oysters  Makes approximately 16 servings

*A delightful, old-timey hors d'oeuvre.*

1 quart standard oysters and their liquor

2 T sugar

1 tsp salt

¼ cup white wine vinegar

¼ cup fresh lemon juice

2 T dry sherry

8 whole cloves

8 whole peppercorns

½ tsp whole allspice

Slices of lemon

Cocktail forks or toothpicks for serving

Place the oysters and their liquor into a medium saucepan. Simmer over medium heat until the oysters begin to curl around the edges, about 3 minutes. Remove the oysters with a slotted spoon and set them aside to cool, keeping liquor in saucepan. Add next 5 ingredients to liquor. Simmer over low for 10 minutes. Remove from heat and cool completely.

Place oysters, cloves, peppercorns, allspice and lemon slices into a container with a cover. Line a sieve with a coffee filter and set it directly over the bowl of oysters; pour in the pickling liquid. Cover tightly and refrigerate for at least 24 hours to allow the flavors to meld.

# Topping oyster dressing   Makes 12 servings

*A Thanksgiving treat that's the tops for those who love cornbread and oysters.*

6 T unsalted butter

1 large sweet onion, minced

5 cups crumbled, day old cornbread, or 1 batch Piney River Cornbread made without fresh corn or sugar, (page 20)

4 cups ½-inch bread cubes made from a stale country loaf

1 ½ tsp dried thyme

1 quart shucked fresh Virginia select oysters

Up to 4 cups of low-salt chicken or turkey stock

3 eggs, well beaten

1 tsp salt

2 tsp freshly ground pepper

Place a large skillet over medium heat. Melt the butter and add the onion and cook, stirring, until the onion is translucent, about 8 minutes. Remove from heat. In a large bowl, combine the corn bread, white bread, the contents of the skillet, thyme, salt and pepper, and set aside. Pour the contents of the jar of oysters through a sieve into a bowl, thus separating the oysters from the liquor. Combine the oyster liquor with enough stock to make 4 cups of liquid. Add the eggs to the liquid, mix well, and set aside.

Preheat the oven to 350 degrees. Butter a very large casserole or baking dish. Spoon half of the bread mixture into the dish. Evenly distribute half of the oysters over top of it. Spoon the remaining bread mixture over top and distribute the rest of the oysters on top. Pour the reserved liquid over the top of the dressing and tightly cover it with a sheet of aluminum foil, dull side out. Place the baking dish on a cookie sheet. Bake for 1 hour. About 15 minutes before serving, remove the foil from the dressing. When the top is nicely browned, remove it from the oven and serve immediately.

# Pear chopped salad  Makes 6 servings

*Sweet and bitter combine in this cascade of flavor. Firm pears are best when cutting into matchsticks.*

2 cups red cabbage, sliced very thinly

2 cups frisée or romaine, chopped

1 bulb fennel, cored and sliced thinly

2 medium pears, cored and chopped into matchsticks

2 tsp chopped fresh thyme

½ cup walnuts toasted and chopped

½ cup crumbled Virginia goat cheese

### Vinaigrette

1 shallot, minced

1 tsp Dijon mustard

1 tsp honey

2 T champagne vinegar

¼ cup walnut oil

Salt and pepper

Combine cabbage, frisée, fennel, pears, and thyme in a salad bowl.

Make vinaigrette: Stir together shallot, mustard, honey, and vinegar. Drizzle in walnut oil, stirring well. Add salt and pepper to taste. Toss salad with vinaigrette. Scatter walnuts and cheese on top.


# Molly's popovers  Makes 12 popovers

*A festive accompaniment to any special meal.*

Softened butter for greasing the pan

4 eggs, at room temperature

1 cup milk, at room temperature

4 T water

4 T unsalted butter, melted

1 cup all-purpose flour

½ tsp salt

Preheat the oven to 375 degrees. Generously grease a 12-hole popover pan or muffin tin with softened butter. Place the pan in the oven to preheat 5 minutes before filling. Whisk together the eggs, milk, water, and melted butter until smooth. Add flour and salt and whisk until smooth. The batter will be thin. Remove the preheated pan from the oven and quickly fill the popover pans less than half full. Bake for 35 minutes. Caution: Do not open the oven to look at them as they bake, lest they fall. Serve immediately with butter and honey or jam.

### DOVE OR QUAIL

Clean and split birds down the back; open flat. Salt and pepper both sides thoroughly. Place flat in large iron frying pan with ⅛ inch butter covering the bottom. Brown on both sides with cover on for 10 minutes. Add one wineglass good red wine to hot pan. Recover, place in 250° oven 10-20 minutes.

Recipe from the original *A Taste of Virginia*

# Pork with apple cider sauce Makes 4 servings

*Substitute roasted sweet potato medallions for a delicious vegetarian entrée.*

4 boneless heirloom pork chops

1 T olive oil

1 T butter

1 red onion sliced thinly

1 heirloom apple, cored, quartered and cut into thin slices

½ cup Virginia apple cider

¼ cup Laird's Old Apple Brandy, or Laird's Applejack

½ cup chicken stock

4 T fresh sage, chopped

½ cup half-and-half or cream

2 T Dijon mustard

Salt and pepper

Salt and pepper pork on both sides. In a large skillet heat olive oil over medium high heat. Brown chops 6 minutes on each side. Transfer to plate.

In same pan, melt butter, add onion, apple, salt and pepper, and sauté until apple starts to brown, stirring occasionally. Add apple cider and apple brandy and simmer about 3 minutes. Add stock, sage and pork juices. Cook another 3 minutes. Stir in half-and-half and mustard and return pork to skillet until finished cooking, about 5 minutes.

# Barbour-q sauce Makes about 3 cups

*Great with shredded pork and chicken. Try it with grated and briefly sautéed sweet potatoes.*

1 minced yellow onion

½ cup apple cider vinegar

½ cup water

1 cup ketchup

2 T Worcestershire sauce

1 T dry mustard

2 T dark brown sugar

Salt and pepper

Combine all ingredients in a medium saucepan and simmer for 25 minutes.

# Brussels sprouts with chestnuts Makes 6 servings

*Crunchy sprouts and creamy chestnuts—totally festive and delectable.*

2 T unsalted butter

1 T walnut oil

1 ½ pounds Brussels sprouts, stems trimmed, any brown leaves discarded, and each sprout thinly sliced, not quartered

Salt and freshly ground pepper to taste

1 5.2 ounce package of whole roasted and peeled chestnuts

In a large lidded skillet, melt butter over medium heat. Add walnut oil. Turn heat to high and add Brussels sprouts. Stir for 2 minutes until browning starts to occur. Turn heat down to low, and place lid on. After 3 minutes, look to see how they're coming and every 2 minutes after that. Do not overcook. When sprouts are bright green, with dark crunchy spots, after about 8 minutes total, turn off the heat. Add salt and pepper and the chestnuts, stir well to combine and serve.

Barboursville Ruins

# Bourbon sweet potato pudding Makes 6 - 8 servings

*A favorite Thanksgiving casserole without the marshmallows.*

6 medium sweet potatoes

1 cup light brown sugar

⅓ cup all-purpose flour

6 T unsalted butter, cold

1 cup chopped pecans

2 large eggs, beaten

2 tsp vanilla

½ cup half-and-half

¼ cup bourbon

¼ teaspoon cinnamon

Place the potatoes in a large pot and cover with salted water. Bring to a boil, reduce heat to medium, cover and cook until very soft, about 30 minutes. Drain and leave to cool.

Combine the sugar and flour and cut in the butter with a fork or pastry cutter. Add the pecans and stir until well blended. Set aside.

Preheat the oven to 350 degrees. Peel the potatoes and mash in a large mixing bowl. Add the eggs, vanilla, half-and-half, bourbon, and cinnamon and mix until well blended. Place potato mixture in a large buttered casserole dish and then top with the pecan topping. Bake until crunchy and brown, about 30 minutes.

Westover Plantation

# Legendary chocolate cake Makes one 10-inch cake

*Richmond's oldest brewery, Legend, makes the brilliant brown ale that is the secret ingredient of this moist, tender cake.*

Parchment paper

Butter for pan

1 cup Legend Brown Ale

10 T unsalted butter

¾ cup unsweetened dutch process cocoa

2 cups sugar

¾ cup sour cream

2 eggs

2 T vanilla

2 cups all-purpose flour

2 ½ tsp baking soda

1 tsp salt

## Frosting

1 ¼ cups confectioners sugar

8 ounces cream cheese, softened

½ cup heavy cream

1 tsp vanilla

Line a 10-inch springform pan with parchment paper. Butter it and set aside. Preheat the oven to 350 degrees. Place brown ale and butter in a medium saucepan over medium heat. Once the butter has melted, remove it from heat. Whisk in the cocoa and sugar.

Whisk sour cream, eggs and vanilla together in a small bowl. Add to the brown ale mixture, followed by the flour, baking soda and salt. Whisk until smooth. Pour into prepared pan and bake until a toothpick inserted in the center comes out clean, about 45 minutes. Place on a rack and cool.

Make the frosting: mix the sugar and cream cheese until smooth. Add cream and vanilla and mix.

Release cake from pan and frost the top and serve.

# Blue Ridge apple cake  Makes 12 servings

*A tried and true favorite to celebrate fall fruit: apples or pears.*

2 cups sugar

1 ¼ cups vegetable oil

3 cups all-purpose flour

3 eggs

1 tsp soda

1 tsp salt

1 tsp cinnamon

2 tsp vanilla

1 ½ cup pecans

### Glaze

2 T unsalted butter

4 T apple cider

½ cup packed light brown sugar

½ tsp salt

2 tsp vanilla extract

1 cup confectioners sugar, sifted

3 medium tart Virginia heirloom apples, peeled, cored and coarsely chopped, about 3 cups

Preheat oven to 350 degrees. Grease and flour a bundt or tube pan. If using an intricate bundt pan, make a paste with shortening and flour and work into nooks and crannies.

In a large bowl, mix sugar and oil with an electric mixer. Add remaining ingredients, except nuts and apples, and mix for 2 minutes. Dough will be stiff. Fold in nuts and apples. Pour into prepared pan. Bake until a tester comes out clean, about an hour. Let cool for 10 minutes on a rack. Invert onto plate.

To make the glaze, melt the butter with the cider in a saucepan, add brown sugar and salt. Stir until sugar is dissolved. Remove from heat. Add vanilla. Slowly whisk in confectioner's sugar. Add more for thicker glaze. Drizzle over warm cake.


# Ginger pear crumble  Makes 4 servings

*An easy, every-day dessert, good enough for special occasions.*

4 pounds ripe pears cored and sliced into chunks

2 lemons, divided: zest of both lemons and 4 T juice

2 T sugar

¾ cup light brown sugar, firmly packed

1 cup all-purpose flour

1 tsp salt

2 tsp grated fresh ginger

½ cup cold unsalted butter, cut into pieces

Whipped cream or ice cream for serving

Preheat oven to 400 degrees. Butter a 9-by-12-inch baking dish. Place pears in a bowl and toss with lemon juice and sugar.

In a medium bowl combine brown sugar, flour, salt, lemon zest, and ginger. Cut butter into sugar mixture until mixture is crumbled to the size of peas. Spoon pears in prepared dish and crumble topping over pears.

Bake for 35 minutes or until lightly browned. Serve with whipped cream.

inter

*Polystichum polyblepharum*
*2015. A.B.T.*

Bottom Opposite Page: George Washington's Mount Vernon, Top: Lewis Ginter Botanical Garden,
Bottom : Courtesy University of Virginia

# Crab Mornay   Makes 48 hors d'oeuvres

*A dear, old favorite from the original* A Taste of Virginia

6 T butter

1 medium onion, minced

½ pound fresh mushrooms, chopped small

4 T flour

1 cup chicken broth

1 cup cream

6 ounces Gruyere cheese, grated

4 ounces Parmesan cheese, grated

Dry sherry to taste

Salt and a pinch of cayenne pepper

2 pounds fresh lump crabmeat

½ cup flat leaf parsley, finely chopped

Siljan's Croustades Cups, roasted mushroom caps or chafing dish for serving

Melt butter in a large skillet. Add onion and mushrooms and sauté over medium heat until onions are translucent but not brown, about 8 minutes. Add flour and stir for one minute. Start adding chicken broth, a bit at a time, stirring constantly until a smooth sauce has been created. Add cream and grated cheeses and stir until cheese is melted. Add sherry, salt and cayenne. Fold in crab meat and parsley.

# Cocktail cheese wafers   Makes 6 dozen wafers

*A perfect cocktail lagniappe.*

1 cup unsalted butter, room temperature

5 ounces of extra-sharp cheddar cheese, finely grated, room temperature

3 ounces Parmigiano-Reggiano cheese, finely grated, room temperature

⅛ tsp cayenne pepper (optional)

2 cups all purpose flour

70 pecan halves

Preheat oven to 350 degrees. Combine the butter, cheeses and cayenne in a large bowl. Mix until well blended. Add the flour gradually and mix until smooth. Roll the dough into 1-inch balls. Place on ungreased baking sheets about an inch apart. Press a pecan half into the center of each one and bake until lightly browned but still fairly soft, about 20 minutes. Remove to a rack and allow to fully cool. Store the wafers in an airtight container.

## WESTMORELAND CLUB EGGNOG

12 eggs, separated
12 dessertspoons sugar
1 quart cream

1 fifth of good bourbon
¼ cup each apple brandy
   and dark rum
grated nutmeg

Beat egg yolks until thick and lemon-colored; sprinkle in sugar, one spoonful at a time, beating constantly. Add liquor in thin stream, still beating. (You may vary the proportion of liquors according to taste. It all depends on what you like, or what you happen to have handy.) Whip the cream, not too stiff, and fold in. (You may add the cream without whipping it, or substitute half and half for a less murderous potion.) Beat egg whites to soft-peak stage and fold in. If it seems too thick or too strong, add some milk. Grate nutmeg generously over the top and put in the icebox to ripen for a week at least. It improves with age.

*Recipe from the original* A Taste of Virginia

Shirley Plantation

# Urbanna oyster stew  Makes 6 to 8 servings

Creamy, rich and wonderful.

7 T unsalted butter, divided

1 medium onion, minced

3 T all-purpose flour

5 cups milk

2 cups heavy cream

1 quart select oysters and their liquor, separated

Salt and freshly ground black pepper

Pinch of cayenne pepper

Sherry to taste, if desired

Oyster crackers to serve

Melt 4 tablespoons of the butter over medium heat in a Dutch oven or large saucepan. Add the onion and some salt and cook, stirring until the onion is translucent, about 10 minutes. Add the flour and cook while stirring for one minute. Whisk in the milk, cream and oyster liquor. Bring to a light simmer, stirring frequently. Do not boil. In a large skillet at medium heat, melt the remaining butter and place the oysters in a single layer. Season with salt and pepper, and cook just until the gills curl. Transfer the contents of the pan to the Dutch oven. Add the cayenne and sherry, if using, and simmer for about 5 minutes. Turn off the heat and serve immediately.

George Washington's Mount Vernon

# Stuffed winter squash  Makes 6 servings

*These beautiful squash can be easily turned into a stunning vegetarian entrée by substituting chopped apple for the sausage.*

3 winter squash, such as acorn or delicata (about 1 pound each), halved lengthwise and seeded

Extra virgin olive oil

½ pound sage sausage

1 cup diced red onion

6 T dried tart cherries or cranberries

¾ cup toasted chopped pecans

2 cups cooked wild rice

½ cup minced scallions

Shagbark hickory syrup or maple syrup to taste

Salt and pepper

Preheat oven to 425 degrees. Brush cut side of squash with olive oil and roast cut side down on a baking sheet for 20-30 minutes or until a fork pierces the squash easily. While the squash is cooking, brown sausage with onions. Stir in cherries, pecans, rice, and scallions. Remove from heat. Add salt and pepper to taste. Plate squash cut side up. Fill with stuffing, drizzle with syrup and serve.

## EASTERN SHORE SWEET POTATO BISCUITS

3 cups sweet potatoes
  boiled and mashed
½ cup lard or butter
2 cups flour

1 teaspoon salt
2 tablespoons sugar
2 teaspoons baking
  powder

Mix while potatoes are still hot. Sift dry ingredients together. Add shortening to hot potatoes, then dry ingredients. Roll out—not too thin—they do not rise much. Preheat oven to 400°, bake 20 minutes. Cook only what you want to eat at once, store rest covered in refrigerator until needed. Butter while hot, serve with Virginia ham.

*Recipe from the original A Taste of Virginia*

# Venison chili  Makes 6 servings

4 slices smoked bacon, chopped

2 pounds venison, freshly ground

1 large onion, chopped

2 cloves garlic, peeled and chopped

2 tsp cumin

4 tsp chili powder

2 tsp smoked paprika

1 (14.5-ounce) can fire-roasted diced tomatoes

2 T tomato paste

1-2 large bottles Legend Brown Ale

Salt and pepper

2 cups cooked kidney beans, drained and rinsed

Grated sharp cheddar cheese and chopped scallions for serving

In a large soup pot, fry bacon over medium heat. Add ground venison and brown. Add onion and garlic and continue to cook for 5-7 minutes. Add spices and cook for 5 more minutes. Stir in tomatoes, tomato paste, and ale. Salt and pepper to taste. Turn heat to low and simmer for 3 hours or until venison is tender. Add more ale as needed. Stir in beans. Serve in bowls. Top with cheese and scallions.

## BEATEN OR THIN BISCUITS

2 cups flour
1 teaspoon salt

4 ounces butter
½ cup ice water

Use food processor with metal blade to mix dough for new versions of two traditional delicacies. Cut butter into small pieces. Put flour and salt into work bowl, turn on and off twice. Add butter and process until mixture looks like corn meal. With machine running, pour ice water through tube. Process for two minutes after mixture forms a ball.

*Beaten Biscuits:* Preheat oven to 350°. Roll dough on lightly floured board to ⅛ inch thick rectangle. Fold in half, making 2 layers. Cut into 1½ inch rounds. Bake on ungreased sheet 25-30 minutes. Makes 36.

*Thin Biscuits:* Chill dough thoroughly. Roll half at a time. Roll paper-thin, cut into rounds and bake as above until barely brown, about 10 minutes. Makes 80 blistery crackers.

Recipe from the original *A Taste of Virginia*

## HASH
*(chicken, turkey, beef or duck – serves 8)*

2 cups leftover meat, cut up
2 onions chopped
1 cup celery chopped
1 cup mushrooms
2 tablespoons butter

2 tablespoons flour
1 cup chicken or beef broth
chopped parsley
salt and pepper

Melt butter. Sauté onions, mushrooms and celery about five minutes. Add meat, sprinkle with flour, stir well. Add broth, stir till thickened and smooth. Season to taste.

Any kind of hash with batter bread is good for lunch or supper, as well as breakfast.

Recipe from the original *A Taste of Virginia*

# POUND CAKE

½ lb. butter
½ cup Crisco
3 cups sugar
5 eggs
3 cups all-purpose flour
1 cup milk

½ teaspoon baking powder
¼ teaspoon salt
2 teaspoons vanilla, or
2 teaspoons almond extract, or
1 teaspoon of each, or
1 teaspoon mace, 1 vanilla

Sift together flour, salt and baking powder three times. Cream butter, Crisco and sugar. Add eggs, beating after each. Add flour, baking powder and salt alternately with milk and flavorings. Pour batter into greased and floured tube or bundt pan and one small loaf pan. Put into cold oven. Turn oven on to 300°, bake 1½ hours. Cool in pans 10 minutes, then take out of pans and cool completely on cake rack.

For Rose-flavored Pound Cake, substitute the following flavorings:

1 teaspoon lemon extract          4 drops rose oil
1 tablespoon grated lemon rind steeped in 1 tablespoon brandy

Recipe from the original *A Taste of Virginia*

# Peppermint ice cream with dark chocolate sauce

### Ice cream   Makes 3 quarts

2 cups milk

1 cup sugar

2 T corn syrup

½ tsp salt

2 cups half-and-half

1 T vanilla extract

4 cups whipping cream

1 ½ cups crushed candy canes

Scald the milk. Remove from heat and add sugar, corn syrup and salt, stirring until dissolved. Stir in half-and-half, vanilla and cream. Cover and refrigerate until cold. Make in batches in ice cream machine. according to manufacturer's instructions, adding candies when ice cream is partially frozen. Transfer to a freezer-safe container and freeze at least 2 hours.

### Dark chocolate sauce   Makes 1 ¼ cups

¾ cup heavy cream          6 ounces bittersweet chocolate          1 tsp vanilla extract

Heat cream and chocolate in a small saucepan over medium heat, whisking until smooth. Add vanilla and serve warm.

George Washington's Mount Vernon

# Eggnog bread pudding with hard sauce Makes 6 servings

1 pound loaf stale brioche bread, in 1-inch cubes

Butter for the pan

1 cup toasted pecans halves

5 eggs

3 cups eggnog*

2 tsp vanilla extract

¼ tsp nutmeg

1 tsp cinnamon

Place bread into a 2-quart buttered baking dish and sprinkle with pecans. Combine liquid ingredients, nutmeg and cinnamon. Stir well and pour over the bread mixture. Allow to sit for 45 minutes. Preheat oven to 350 degrees and bake for about 40 minutes until firm. Serve with hard sauce.

* If using non-alcoholic eggnog, add ¼ cup brandy.

## Hard sauce

½ cup butter

½ cup sugar

4 beaten egg yolks

Pinch of salt

1 cup cream

1 ½ ounces brandy

Cream butter and sugar together. When light and creamy, add egg yolks, salt, cream, and brandy. Cook in a double boiler stirring constantly until thick. Serve immediately.

# The Gardens of Virginia

As of July 2018

Restored by the Garden Club of Virginia with funding from Historic Garden Week tours

www.GCVirginia.org

**Bacon's Castle**
Surry

**Belle Grove**
Middletown

**Belmont**
Fredericksburg

**Bruton Parish Church**
Williamsburg

**Burwell-Morgan Mill**
Millwood

**Centre Hill Mansion**
Petersburg

**Christ Church - Lancaster**
Irvington

**Danville Museum of Fine Arts and History**
Danville

**Executive Mansion Capitol Square**
Richmond

**Fincastle Presbyterian Church**
Fincastle

**Grace Arents Garden at Lewis Ginter Botanical Garden**
Richmond

**Green Spring Gardens**
Alexandria

**Historic Henry County Courthouse**
Martinsville

**Historic Portsmouth Courthouse**
Portsmouth

**Hollins University**
Roanoke

**John Handley High School**
Winchester

**Kenmore**
Fredericksburg

**Kent-Valentine House**
Richmond

**Ker Place**
Onancock

**Lee Hall**
Newport News

**Mary Washington House**
Fredericksburg

**Mary Washington Monument**
Fredericksburg

**Maymont**
Richmond

**Monticello**
Charlottesville

**Montpelier**
Montpelier Station

**Moses Myers House**
Norfolk

**Mount Vernon**
Mount Vernon

**Oatlands**
Leesburg

**Poe Museum**
Richmond

**Point of Honor**
Lynchburg

**Poplar Forest**
Forest

**Smith's Fort**
Surry

**St. John's Mews**
Richmond

**State Arboretum of Virginia- Blandy Experimental Farm**
Boyce

**Stratford Hall**
Stratford

**Sweet Briar College**
Sweet Briar

**University of Virginia**
Charlottesville

**Washington and Lee University**
Lexington

**Wilton**
Richmond

**Woodrow Wilson Presidential Library**
Staunton

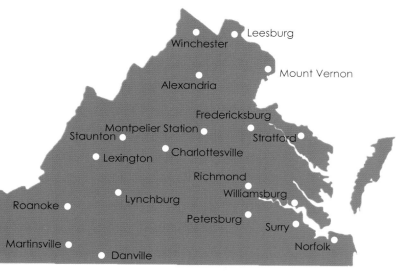